STEM
Waterworks

How Do SEWERS Work?

Greg Roza

PowerKiDS press

New York

Published in 2017 by The Rosen Publishing Group, Inc.
29 East 21st Street, New York, NY 10010

First Edition

Editor: Greg Roza
Book Design: Mickey Harmon

Photo Credits: Cover, pp. 1–32 (water) elic/Shutterstock.com; cover (image) Hunstock/Getty Images pp. 1–32 (pipes) Kovalenko Alexander/Shutterstock.com; cover (image) Huntstock/Getty Images; p. 5 ADRIAN DENNIS/Staff/AFP/Getty Images; p. 7 Merten Snijders/Getty Images; p. 9 De Agostini/C. Sappa/De Agostini Picture Library/Getty Images; p. 11 Heritage Images/Contributor/Hulton Archive/ Getty Images; p. 13 Anatoli Styf/Shutterstock.com; p. 15 Kletr/Shutterstock.com; p. 17 (sky) detchana wangkheeree/Shutterstock.com; p. 17 (diagram) AuntSpray/Shutterstock.com; p. 19 (trap) Science & Society Picture Library/Contributor/SSPL/Getty Images; p. 19 (terra-cotta pipes) steve estvanik/ Shutterstock.com; p. 19 (main) Toa55/Shutterstock.com; p. 21 Jim Vallee/Shutterstock.com; p. 23 (inset) Alexey Khromushin/Shutterstock.com; p. 23 (main) KUPRYNENKO ANDRII/Shutterstock.com; p. 25 https://commons.wikimedia.org/wiki/File:The_vision_of_a_toilet_that_is_small_-_and_pleasant_-_ enough_to_fit_inside_someone%27s_home_(prototype_but_not_fully_functional)_(13359389583).jpg; p. 27 Avatar_023/Shutterstock.com; p. 29 Andrew Burton/Staff/Getty Image News/Getty Images.

Library of Congress Cataloging-in-Publication Data

Names: Roza, Greg, author.
Title: How do sewers work? / Greg Roza.
Description: New York : PowerKids Press, [2016] | Series: STEM
  waterworks | Includes index.
Identifiers: LCCN 2016013446 | ISBN 9781499420036 (pbk.) | ISBN 9781499420050 (library bound) | ISBN 9781499420043 (6 pack)
Subjects: LCSH: Sewerage–Design and construction–Juvenile literature. |
  Storm sewers–Juvenile literature. | Sanitary engineering–Juvenile
  literature.
Classification: LCC TD745 .R69 2016 | DDC 628.2–dc23
LC record available at http://lccn.loc.gov/2016013446

Manufactured in the United States of America

CPSIA Compliance Information: Batch #BS16PK: For Further Information contact Rosen Publishing, New York, New York at 1-800-237-9932

Contents

Sewer STEM

You have probably heard your teachers talk about STEM, which stands for science, technology, engineering, and mathematics. These subjects play an important role in how our world has been shaped, and what the future will be like. STEM affects so much in our lives—from the foods we eat to the games we play. It even plays a role in how we eliminate wastewater from our lives.

Few people want to think about how sewer systems work; we just want them to work! However, for centuries, scientists and engineers have constructed and improved upon sewer systems with new technology. Thanks to professionals who spend time thinking about sewage and sewer systems, our world has become a much healthier and cleaner place to live.

This sewer technician removes fat from a London sewer tunnel. People wash animal fat from cooking down their drains. This leads to the buildup of fat in sewer systems, which causes major problems.

In the Pipe

Before sewer systems existed, many growing cities were dirty, smelly places. Garbage and human waste were often dumped in the streets. This led to terrible illnesses, such as cholera, in 19th-century Europe.

Kinds of Sewer Systems

Sewer systems are designed to carry wastewater away from homes and buildings. They're made up of basic parts including pipes, tunnels, and drains. Many sewers are designed to use gravity to move wastewater downhill. This reduces the amount of energy needed to move the wastewater. Other sewer systems need pumps to move wastewater from a low point to a higher point.

Early sewers were generally open sewers. That means wastewater is led away from populated areas using open trenches or canals. However, this can cause a lot of problems for people and the **environment**. Open sewers have been largely replaced by closed, or **sanitary**, sewers, which use enclosed pipes and tunnels. A combined sewer is a sanitary sewer that also collects rainwater and runoff water.

Open sewers are still used in parts of the world where people can't afford modern sewers. This results in the spread of pests and diseases.

First Flushes

Most early civilizations grew near rivers, lakes, and oceans. Bodies of water provided means of travel, food, and water for drinking and bathing. They were also commonly used as a place to dump garbage as well as human and animal waste. People didn't realize they were **contaminating** the water with dangerous illnesses.

Most ancient societies had very simple sewer systems. The first organized systems designed to carry waste away from communities were simple open trenches. As early as 4000 BC, the ancient Babylonians began making clay pipes to move wastewater away from homes. The ancient Minoans had plumbing, too. The royal palace at Knossos had a toilet on the ground floor and a rooftop tank that collected rainwater. This water was used to flush the toilet.

In the Pipe

Venice is a beautiful, old Italian city with canals instead of streets. People use boats to get around. However, Venice's canal system is also its sewage removal system. Modern engineers are searching for ways to improve this system to protect people and the environment from harm.

The ancient Romans built amazing structures of all kinds, including aqueducts to bring freshwater into cities and trenches that took wastewater out of cities. Like other ancient civilizations, the Romans also had public **latrines** and bathhouses.

Bazalgette and Snow Save London

One of the first modern sewer systems was constructed in London, England, between 1859 and 1868. During the 19th century, the streets of many European cities were filled with garbage and wastewater. In London, raw sewage began to fill and overflow basements. Londoners decided to start piping the sewage into the Thames River, which is also where they got their drinking water. In the 1850s,

In the Pipe

At first, English scientists believed cholera was spreading through the air. However, a doctor named John Snow discovered that it was being spread from a water pump on Broad Street. Snow worked very hard to prove this to the people of London, and today he's remembered as the father of modern **epidemiology**.

The months of July and August in 1858 were known as the "Great Stink" in London because the city smelled like sewage!

cholera overwhelmed London. To battle the cholera outbreak, scientists decided a system of sewage removal was desperately needed.

Civil engineer Joseph Bazalgette designed and built the new system. It includes tunnels, pipes, and pumps to take sewage farther away from the city so it doesn't contaminate the water supply. Without Bazalgette's **innovative** design, London's cholera problem could have become even worse.

Continued Innovation

After the construction of early sewer systems in Europe, other cities began to build their own systems. Engineers quickly realized the importance of accessing sewer tunnels for inspection and **maintenance**. This resulted in the invention of manholes, which also provided important **ventilation** for sewer systems.

Initially, most modern sewer systems were sanitary sewers that led wastewater away from populations into a body of water. Combined sewer systems collect both wastewater and runoff. Although useful, combined systems don't always work properly during bad rainstorms and when snow melts in the spring. These conditions can fill combined sewer systems and allow sewage to enter the environment and sources of community water. It wasn't long before scientists turned their attention to sewage treatment to protect people and the environment.

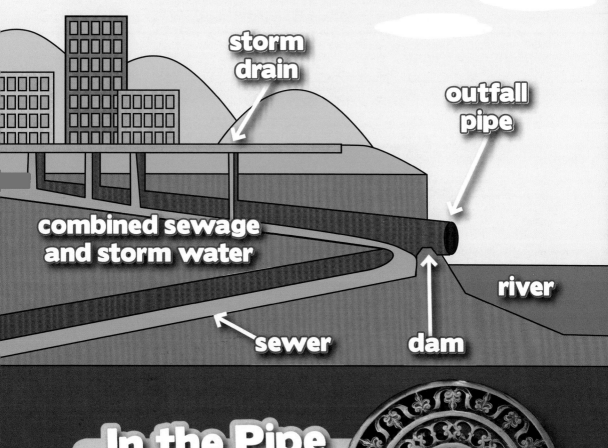

This diagram of a combined sewer system shows how increased runoff is managed. When there is too much runoff, such as during a flood, the dam in a combined sewer may not be sufficient to stop sewage from entering local rivers and lakes. This is bad for the environment.

storm drain

outfall pipe

combined sewage and storm water

river

sewer

dam

In the Pipe

Many manhole covers are plain. Some are decorative. And some are works of art!

In 1914, two English engineers—Edward Ardern and W.T. Lockett—published a paper titled "Experiments on the **Oxidation** of Sewage Without the Aid of Filters." This paper described the activated sludge process for treating wastewater.

Using this process, air and special bacteria are added to wastewater in a large, open tank. The bacteria cause solids, known as floc or sludge, to separate from the wastewater and settle in the tank. The cleaner water is further treated and allowed to flow back into the environment. This process also releases gases, such as nitrogen and carbon dioxide, into the atmosphere. These gases pass through odor treatment technology before being released into the air. The sludge is "recycled" and goes through the activated sludge process again. Today, the activated sludge process is still the most effective wastewater treatment process.

Water treatment plants that use the activated sludge process have large, open tanks where oxygen is forced into the wastewater. This is an aerial view of a large treatment plant in the Czech Republic, Europe.

Septic Science

Some homes use a septic system rather than being connected to a sewer system. A septic system is called a passive system because it's powered by gravity alone. A septic system takes wastewater from a house or another building and stores it in a septic tank below ground. In this tank, solid materials sink to the bottom. Bacteria in the tank break down this organic matter, and this smells really bad! It's a good thing the tank is underground. As the solid matter sinks, relatively clean water is left behind.

As new wastewater enters a septic tank, the older water is forced through pipes into a drain field, also called a leach field. There, the water seeps into the soil. This cleaner wastewater is actually good for lawns.

to leach field   septic tank

after the flush

The wastewater that enters a leach field contains the elements nitrogen and phosphorus, which are both good fertilizers. This is good for your lawn! The leach field needs to be treated or moved after about 15 to 20 years.

Perfecting Pipes

Over the centuries, many materials have been used to make sewer **conduits**. The first pipes were made of wood, terra-cotta, stone, and other simple materials. These pipes often leaked, leading to contaminated soil. They were replaced by cast iron, lead, and clay pipes.

In the early 1900s, American companies developed a conduit made of wood pulp, glue, and tar. These pipes were first used for electrical wires, but they were soon used for plumbing as well. After many years, these pipes are breaking down, which has caused a problem for some American communities.

Companies started using **PVC** pipes in the late 1960s. These sewer and drain pipes have become lighter, stronger, and cheaper since then, making them the most popular choice for sewer conduits.

terra-cotta pipes

PVC pipes

A Buchan trap is a pipe with a dip in the middle that holds water. This is similar to the pipe under the sinks in your house. The water makes a seal that keeps bad smells and rodents from entering homes through sewer pipes.

Vacuum Sewer Systems

The newest sewer system technology is the vacuum system. This system includes pipes that are easy to install and maintain. The water inside a vacuum system moves about 15 to 18 feet (4.6 to 5.5 m) per second. The speed of the wastewater allows it to move uphill. It also helps keep the inside of the pipes clean, which can extend their life.

Gravity starts the process by taking wastewater from a home and storing it in an underground tank. Once the tank has about 10 gallons (37.9 L) in it, the system automatically opens a **valve** leading to a pipe. This pipe "sucks" the wastewater into a central tank. The central tank creates the vacuum that sucks up wastewater.

Vacuum sewers aren't new. The first ones were built during the 1880s in Europe. Modern technology, such as the grinder pump shown here, make vacuum systems even more efficient.

Toilet Tech

Toilets have changed a lot over the years. Ancient toilets were simple seats with holes in them. Waste dropped into a pit or into open trenches to be carried away. Many cultures used chamber pots that needed to be emptied after they were used. In the late 1500s, English poet and amateur engineer John Harington built a new home and installed the first flush toilet in it. He called it the Ajax. Queen Elizabeth I tried it and ordered one for herself! It wasn't until 1775 when another Englishman, Alexander Cumming, received the first patent for a flushing "water closet."

Modern flush toilets were first built with raised tanks. When the toilet was flushed, gravity pulled the water down and took the wastewater away. Toilets today use smaller tanks and are more efficient.

Toilets are becoming more and more high-tech. Some include electronic controls. Some even have heated seats!

ancient
Roman toilets

The WHO/UNICEF Joint Monitoring Programme for Water Supply and Sanitation (JMP)—established by the World Health Organization (WHO) and the United Nations Children's Fund (UNICEF)—studies sanitation facilities and drinking water sources around the world. They found that 32 percent of the world's people lack proper sanitation services. A lack of access to clean toilets and clean drinking water leads to illnesses for thousands of children every day.

In 2011, the Bill & Melinda Gates Foundation announced the Reinvent the Toilet Challenge. This program gives grants to groups that are creating new toilet and sewer technology. The challenge aims to create a toilet that removes germs from human waste, operates without electricity, and costs less than five cents a day to use.

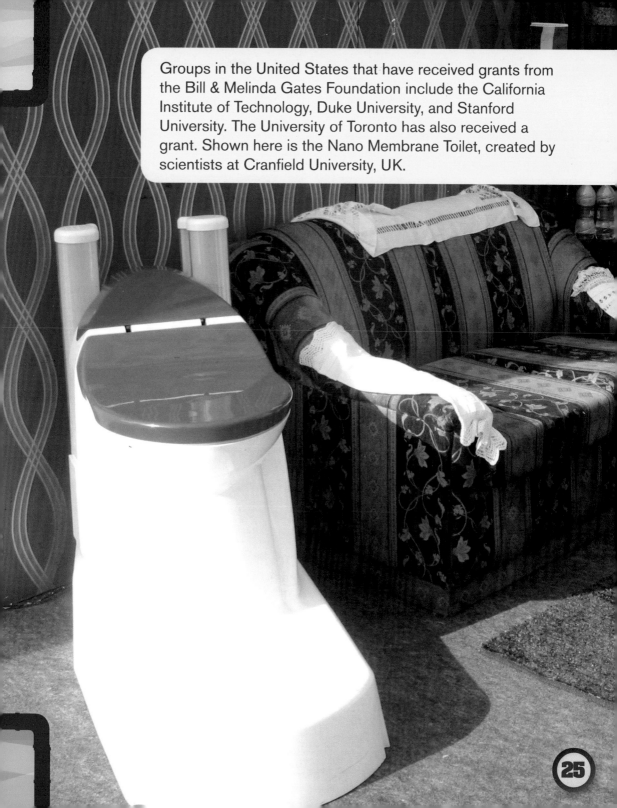

Groups in the United States that have received grants from the Bill & Melinda Gates Foundation include the California Institute of Technology, Duke University, and Stanford University. The University of Toronto has also received a grant. Shown here is the Nano Membrane Toilet, created by scientists at Cranfield University, UK.

Engineering Sewers

Throughout history, civil engineers have helped build our communities, including effective sewer systems. Anyone interested in pursuing a career in this field will need to go to school for civil engineering, **hydraulics** engineering, or environmental engineering.

Environmental engineers help keep the public safe from environmental problems, such as pollution. They help design and build sewers that won't hurt the environment or people. Hydraulics engineers are experts in how water acts and how to protect water resources. In fact, some are known as water resource engineers. Others are known as storm water engineers. All these professionals help make sewer systems that are efficient and effective. Other engineers who might play a part in the construction and maintenance of sewers include geological engineers, mechanical engineers, and facilities engineers.

In the Pipe

Have you ever thought about being a plumber? It may not sound like the cleanest or most exciting job in the world, but it's a career that requires using STEM skills to help customers. Plumbers also earn good money.

This engineer is monitoring water quality in a water treatment plant.

Sewer Math?

What does math have to do with sewer systems? A lot! Scientists use math to discover how a new sewer system will affect a community. They may take measurements of water depth, speed, or levels of contamination.

Engineers use equations to help them determine how much water can flow through a system, or how much energy is needed to power a water pump. For example, wastewater treatment plants are designed to receive a certain amount of water flow a day. During rainy periods, this amount can change greatly. Engineers need to be able to calculate how much water will flow into the facility, which will affect how the facility is constructed. Workers use measurement tools, including tape measures and surveying equipment.

Maintenance workers need math when dealing with sewer systems. When digging wells or septic systems, workers need to be able to calculate surface area and volume before the job begins. They need to estimate the amount of materials that will be required, such as PVC pipes.

Modern Problems, STEM Solutions

Societies have come a long way from the days of chamber pots. Scientists and engineers have faced many sanitation problems and discovered solutions to make our lives easier, cleaner, and safer. However, we still face problems when it comes to waste removal systems. Many areas have systems that are out-of-date and often pose problems for the environment. There are areas of the world where open trenches are still used, and the public health suffers because of this.

Modern sewer systems need to be designed with the health of populations and the environment in mind. It's a dirty job, but someone has to do it. You can thank scientists, engineers, plumbers, and maintenance workers for keeping your toilets flushing smoothly!

Glossary

conduit: A pipe or tube through which something passes.

contaminate: To pollute.

environment: The natural world in which a plant or animal lives.

epidemiology: A branch of medical science that deals with disease in a population.

hydraulics: The science that deals with ways to use liquid (such as water) when it's moving.

innovative: Introducing or using new ideas and methods.

latrine: An outdoor toilet that usually includes a hole in the ground.

maintenance: The act of taking care of something, or maintaining it.

oxidation: The process of combining something with oxygen.

PVC: A very common form of plastic. Short for polyvinyl chloride.

sanitary: Relating to good health or protection from illnesses.

valve: A device that opens and closes to control the flow of a liquid or gas.

ventilation: A means of providing fresh air or removing harmful air.

Index

Websites

Due to the changing nature of Internet links, PowerKids Press has developed an online list of websites related to the subject of this book. This site is updated regularly. Please use this link to access the list: www.powerkidslinks.com/sww/sewe